The Book of

KidsSongs 2

A Holler-Along Handbook
for Home or on the Range

by Nancy and John Cassidy

illustrated by Jim M'Guinness
music produced by Ken Whiteley

Klutz Press ♪ Palo Alto, California

Design, Art Direction and Production:
MaryEllen Podgorski & Suzanne Gooding

Illustrations: Jim M'Guinness

Transcription: Barbara Allen Roberts

Music Production and Direction: Ken Whiteley

Proofreaders: Gary and Shireen Lowman

Special thanks to all my classes at Phillips Brooks, Escondido, and Ohlone Elementary Schools.

Klutz Press is an independent publisher located in Palo Alto, California and staffed entirely by real humans. We would love to hear your comments regarding this or any of our books.

Additional Copies:
For the location of your nearest Klutz retailer, call (415) 857-0888. If they should all be regrettably out of stock, the entire library of Klutz books, as well as a variety of other things we happen to like, are available in our mail order catalogue. To get a copy, write us at: Klutz Press, 2121 Staunton Court, Palo Alto, CA 94306, or call (415) 424-0739.
Order information is also located on the back of the card in the KidsSongs cassette case.

4   1   5

ISBN 0-932592-20-1

Published by Klutz Press
Palo Alto, California

The "book and bag" packaging format is a registered trademark of Klutz Press.

Song List

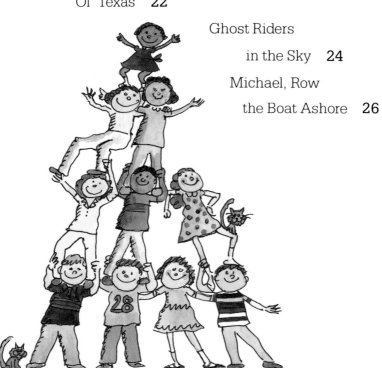

She'll Be Coming Round the Mountain

Traditional

She'll be com-ing round the moun tain when she comes (toot She'll be toot)

com-ing round the moun tain when she comes (toot toot) She'll be

com-ing round the moun-tain, She'll be

com-ing round the moun-tain, She'll be

com-ing round the moun-tain when she comes (toot toot)

She'll be driving 6 white horses when she comes (whoa back),
She'll be driving 6 white horses when she comes (whoa back)
She'll be driving 6 white horses, She'll be driving 6 white horses,
She'll be driving 6 white horses when she comes (whoa back).

Oh, we'll all go out to meet her when she comes (hi babe),
Oh we'll all go out to meet her when she comes (hi babe).
Oh we'll all go out to meet her, We'll all go out to meet her,
We'll all go out to meet her when she comes (hi babe).

6

She'll be wearing red pajamas when she comes
  (scratch, scratch),
She'll be wearing red pajamas when she comes
  (scratch, scratch),
She'll be wearing red pajamas,
She'll be wearing red pajamas,
She'll be wearing red pajamas when she comes
  (scratch, scratch).

She will have to sleep with Grandma when she comes
  (snee snore),
She will have to sleep with Grandma when she comes
  (snee snore),
She will have to sleep with Grandma,
She will have to sleep with Grandma,
She will have to sleep with Grandma when she comes
  (snee snore).
          Scratch scratch, hi babe, whoa back, toot, toot.

Sandwiches

Bob King

Chorus:
Sand-wich-es are beau-ti- ful,

sand-wich-es are fine.

I like sand-wich-es, I eat them all the time; I

eat them for my sup-per and I eat them for my lunch; If I

had a hun-dred sand-wich-es, I'd eat them all at once.

I'm a roaming and a rambling
and a wandering all along,
And if you care to listen,
I will sing a happy song.

I will not ask a favor and I
will not ask a fee,
But if you have a sandwich,
won't you give a bite to me?

CHORUS

Once I went to England,
    I visited the Queen,
I swear she was the grandest
    lady that I've ever seen,
I told her she was beautiful
    and could not ask for more,
She handed me a sandwich
    and she threw me
    out the door.

CHORUS

A sandwich may be egg
    or cheese or
    even peanut butter,
But they all taste so good
    to me,
    it doesn't even matter;
Jam or ham or cucumber,
    any kind will do.
I like sandwiches,
    how about you?

CHORUS

Rig A Jig Jig

Additional lyrics: N. Cassidy

As I was walk-ing down the street,

Down the street, down the street, A

ver-y good friend I chanced to meet; Hi

Ho Hi Ho Hi Ho.

Chorus:
Rig a jig jig and a-way we go, A-

way we go, a- way we go;

Rig a jig jig and a-way we go, Hi

Ho Hi Ho Hi Ho.

We clapped our hands and stomped our feet,
Stomped our feet, stomped our feet,
We clapped our hands and stomped our feet,
Hi Ho Hi Ho Hi Ho.

We jumped up high and came back down,
Came back down, came back down,
We jumped up high and came back down,
Hi Ho Hi Ho Hi Ho.

Rig a jig jig and away we go,
Away we go, away we go,
Rig a jig jig and away we go,
Hi Ho Hi Ho Hi Ho.

We climbed on a train and tooted the horn,
Tooted the horn, tooted the horn,
We climbed on a train and tooted the horn,
Hi Ho Hi Ho Hi Ho.

Kissed my ma and hugged my pa,
Hugged my pa, hugged my pa,
Kissed my ma and hugged my pa,
Hi Ho Hi Ho Hi Ho.

CHORUS

Fooba-Wooba John

Traditional

A

a

Saw a snail chase whale, Foo-ba-woo-ba, foo-ba-woo-ba,

E7   A

Saw a snail chase a whale, Foo - ba - woo - ba   John.

D   A   E7

Saw a snail chase a whale, All a- round the wa- ter pail.

A   E7   A

Hey, John, ho, John, Foo - ba - woo - ba   John.

Saw a frog chase a dog, Fooba-wooba, fooba-wooba.
Saw a frog chase a dog, Fooba-wooba John.
Saw a frog chase a dog, sitting on a hollow log.
Hey, John, ho, John, Fooba-wooba John.

Saw a flea kick a tree,
Fooba-wooba, fooba-wooba.
Saw a flea kick a tree,
Fooba-wooba John.
Saw a flea kick a tree,
In the middle of the sea.
Hey, John, ho, John,
Fooba-wooba John.

Heard a cow say me-ow,
Fooba-wooba, fooba-wooba.
Heard a cow say me-ow,
Fooba-wooba John.
Heard a cow say me-ow,
Then I heard it say bow-wow.
Hey John, ho, John,
Fooba-wooba John.

The Desperado

Additional lyrics: N. & C. Cassidy

Chorus:

For a bold bad man was this des-per-a-do, From

Bad-man's Gulch way down in Col-or-a-do. And he

rode a-round like a big tor-na-do, And

ev-'ry-where he went he gave his BIG whoop—Hey! He

Fine

was a des-per-a-do from the wild and wool-ly West, But

ev-ry now and then he'd go and give the West a rest, He'd

sad-dle up his horse, put on his spurs and leath-er vest, And

D.C. al Fine

ev-'ry-where he went he gave his BIG whoop—Hey!

14

He had a skunk named Arnie but he thought he was a hat,
He'd put him up on top his head and wear him just like that,
And everywhere they'd go the people'd point and say
    what's that,
And Arnie'd wag his tail and give his BIG whoop—HEY!

CHORUS

He had a horse named Lightnin' but she wasn't very quick,
She never liked to run but she could snort and buck and kick,
And when our Desperado saddled up and gave a kick,
She'd throw him so you'd really hear his BIG whoop! Hey!

CHORUS

15

The Bus Song

Traditional

G

The wheels on the bus go round and round,

D7   G

round and round,   round and round.   The

wheels   on the bus   go   round and round,

D7   G

All through the town. ——

The wipers on the bus go, "Swish, swish, swish,
Swish, swish, swish; swish, swish, swish."
The wipers on the bus go, "Swish, swish, swish,"
All through the town.

The horn on the bus goes, "Beep, beep, beep,
Beep, beep, beep; beep, beep beep."
The horn on the bus goes, "Beep, beep, beep,"
All through the town.

The gas on the bus goes, "Glunk, glunk, glunk,
Glunk, glunk, glunk; glunk, glunk, glunk.
The gas on the bus goes, "Glunk, glunk, glunk,"
All through the town.

The money on the bus goes, "Clink, clink, clink,
Clink, clink, clink; clink, clink, clink.
The money on the bus goes, "Clink, clink, clink,"
All through the town.

The baby on the bus says, "Wah, wah, wah!"
Wah, wah, wah! Wah, wah, wah!"
The baby on the bus says "Wah, wah, wah!"
All through the town.

The mommy on the bus says, "I love you,
I love you, I love you."
The daddy on the bus says, "I love you too,"
All through the town.

3QRI2J609

Lavender's Blue

Traditional

Chorus:
Lav- en- der's blue, dil-ly dil-ly, lav- en- der's green,

When you are King, dil-ly dil-ly, I shall be Queen.

Who told you so, dil-ly dil-ly, who told you so?

'Twas my own heart, dil-ly dil-ly, that told me so.

MAKE YOUR OWN
Body Bells

Materials: As many jingle bells and shoelaces as you can get.

Instructions: Tie three or four bells onto each shoelace and have someone tie each jingle bell lace around your wrists, ankles, head, waist, knee, toe, etc...

Call up your friends, dilly dilly,
    set them to work.
Some to the plough, dilly dilly,
    some to the fork;
Some to the hay, dilly dilly,
    some to cut corn;
While you and I, dilly dilly,
    keep ourselves warm.

CHORUS

19

There's a Little Wheel A-Turning in My Heart

Additional lyrics: N. Cassidy

There's a lit-tle wheel a-turn-ing in my heart, There's a

lit- tle wheel a- turn-ing in my   heart. In my

heart, —— In my   heart, —— There's a

lit - tle wheel a- turn-ing in my   heart.

There's a little song a singing in my heart,
There's a little song a singing in my heart,
In my heart, in my heart,
There's a little song a singing in my heart.

There's a little frog a leaping in my heart,
There's a little frog a leaping in my heart,
In my heart, in my heart,
There's a little frog a leaping in my heart.

I see the sun a rising in my heart,
I see the sun a rising in my heart,
In my heart, in my heart,
I see the sun a rising in my heart.

We're dancing round the world in my heart,
We're dancing round the world in my heart,
In my heart, in my heart,
We're dancing round the world in my heart.

Ol' Texas

Traditional

I'm gon - na leave— ol' Tex - as now,—

They've got no use— for the long-horned cow.

They've plowed and fenced— my— cat - tle range,—

And the peo - ple there— are all so strange.

I'll take my horse, I'll take my rope,
And hit the trail upon a lope;
I'll bid Adios to the Alamo,
And turn my head toward Mexico.

Ghost Riders in the Sky

(A COWBOY LEGEND)

Words and Music by
Stan Jones

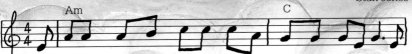

An old cow-poke went rid-ing   one dark   wind-y day, Up-
                                         out   and

on a ridge he rest-ed as he went a-long his way,   When

all at once a might-y herd of red-eyed cows he saw, A -

plow-ing through the rag-ged skies   and up a cloud-y

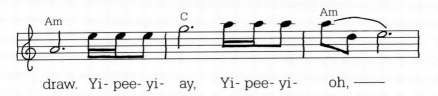

draw. Yi- pee-yi- ay,   Yi- pee-yi- oh, ——

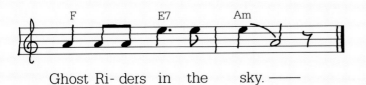

Ghost Ri- ders in the   sky. ——

Their brands were still on fire and their hooves were made of
  steel,
Their horns were black and shiny and their hot breath he
  could feel,
A bolt of fear went through him as they thundered through
  the sky,
For he saw the riders coming hard and heard their mournful
  cry.

Yipee-yi-ay, Yipee-yi-oh, Ghost Riders in the sky.

Their faces gaunt, their eyes were blurred, their shirts were
  soaked with sweat,
They're riding hard to catch that herd but they ain't got'em
  yet.
They have to ride forever on that range up in the sky,
On horses breathing fire, as they ride I hear them cry.

Yipee-yi-ay, Yipee-yi-oh, Ghost Riders in the sky.

The riders loped on by him and he heard one call his name,
"If you want to save your hide and soul a-ridin on this range
Then cowboy change your ways today or with us you will ride,
Trying to catch the devil's herd across the endless sky."

Yipee-yi-ay, Yipee-yi-oh, Ghost Riders in the sky.

25

Michael
Row the Boat Ashore

Traditional
Verse 1: Cody Cassidy

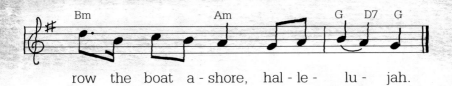

Mi-chael, row the boat a-shore, hal-le-lu-jah, Mi-chael,

row the boat a-shore, hal-le-lu-jah.

My brothers and sisters are all aboard, hallelujah;
My brothers and sisters are all aboard, hallelujah.
Michael row the boat ashore, hallelujah;
Michael row the boat ashore, hallelujah.

The river is deep and the river is wide, hallelujah;
Milk and honey on the other side, hallelujah.
Michael row the boat ashore, hallelujah;
Michael row the boat ashore, hallelujah.

Jordan's river is chilly and cold, hallelujah;
Chills the body but warms the soul, hallelujah.
Michael row the boat ashore, hallelujah;
Michael row the boat
ashore, hallelujah.

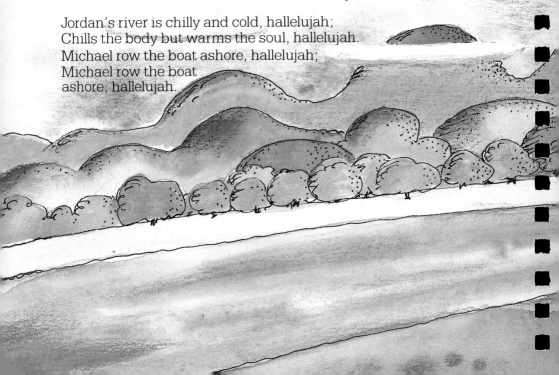

La Bamba

Traditional
English lyrics: N. Cassidy

Bam-ba bam-ba,   bam-ba bam-ba,   Bam-ba bam-

ba, Pa-ra bai-lar la bam-ba,   pa-ra bai-lar la   bam-

ba Se ne-ces- si- ta un-a po-ca de gra- cia,

Un-a po-ca de gra-ci-a, y o-tra co- si- ta, Ar-ri-ba ar-

ri-ba,   y ar-ri- ba ar- ri-ba, Ar-ri-ba i-re

por-ti se-re,   por-ti se- re.

Bamba bamba, bamba bamba,
   bamba bamba.
Let's dance with the music,
Let's dance with the music.
When we dance we sing a song,
We sing a song of thanks,
And clap our hands and we go
Faster and faster, higher and higher,
louder and louder.

   Repeat first verse.

Bamba bamba, bamba bamba,
      bamba bamba.
Softer and softer—
      bamba la bamba—
         bamba!

Boom, Boom, Ain't It Great to Be Crazy

Traditional; 2nd verse J. Cassidy

Chorus:
Boom, Boom ain't it great to be cra - zy, Boom,

Boom ain't great to be cra - zy,

Gid - dy and fool - ish all day long, Boom,

Boom, ain't it great to be cra - zy.

Fine

Way down South where ba - nan - as grow, A

flea stepped on an el - e - phant's toe. The

el - e - phant cried with tears in his eyes,

D.C. al Fine

"Why don't you pick on some-one your own size?"

CHORUS

Late last night I had a real strange dream,
Ate a nine pound marshmallow momma gave me.
When I woke up I knew something was wrong,
I looked around, saw my pillow was gone.

CHORUS

31

Cluck, Cluck, Red Hen

Jackie Reinach

Baa, baa, black sheep, have you an - y wool?

Yes sir, yes sir, three bags full,

Fine

One for your sweat-er and one for your rug,

D.C. al Fine

One for your blank-et to keep you warm and snug.

Cluck, cluck red hen, have you any eggs?
Yes sir, yes sir, as many as your legs,
One for your breakfast and one for your lunch,
Come back tomorrow I'll have another bunch.

Moo, moo, brown cow have you milk for me?
Yes sir, yes sir, as tasty as can be,
Churn it into butter, make it into cheese,
Freeze it into ice cream or drink it if you please.

Buzz, buzz, busy bee, is your honey sweet?
Yes sir, yes sir, sweet enough to eat,
Honey on your muffin, honey on your cake,
Honey by the spoonful, as much as I can make.

Baa, baa, black sheep, have you any wool?
Yes sir, yes sir, three bags full.

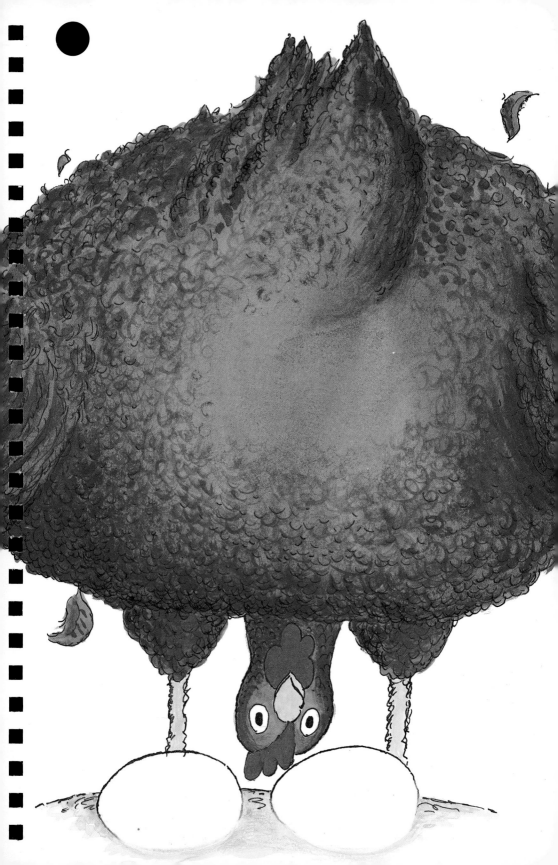

Hey Dum Diddley Dum

Marc Stone
Additional lyrics: J. Cassidy

Chorus:
Hey dum did-dl-ey dum, Hey dum did-dl-ey dum

Hey dum did-dl-ey, Hey dum did-dl-ey, Hey dum did-dl-ey dum.

> C'mon and sing along,
> I've got the world's most singable song,
> It's got a hey and a hum and a did-dl-ey dum,
> And I hope you'll sing along.
>
> CHORUS

It's a kind of help-along song,
It can help you out when things go wrong.
When you're feeling sad, and your day's gone bad,
Sing Hey dum did-dl-ey dum.

CHORUS

MAKE YOUR OWN
Kitchen Drums

Materials: Big collection of pots and pans, two wooden spoons.

Instructions: Clear out any grown-ups, turn the pots and pans upside down and set them up in front of you, then bang away.

Old Chisholm Trail

Traditional

Well, come a-long friends,   lis- ten to my tale; I'll

tell you my trou-bles on the old Chis-olm trail. Come-a

ti   yi yip-py, yip-py, yay, yip-py yay! Come - a

ti   yi   yip - py   yip - py   yay!

On a ten-dollar horse, a forty-dollar saddle;
I started out a-punchin' those long-horned cattle.
Come-a ti yi yippy, yippy, yay, yippy yay!
Come-a ti yi yippy, yippy, yay!

I'm up in the morning before daylight;
Before I get to sleep the moon's shining bright.

Come-a ti yi yippy, yippy, yay, yippy yay!
Come-a ti yi yippy, yippy, yay!

It's bacon and beans 'most every day,
I'd sooner be a-eatin' the prairie hay.

Come-a ti yi yippy, yippy, yay, yippy yay!
Come-a ti yi yippy, yippy, yay!

I'll sell my outfit as soon as I can,
'Cause I ain't punchin' cattle for no mean
   boss man.

Come-a ti yi yippy, yippy, yay, yippy yay!
Come-a ti yi yippy, yippy, yay!

With my knees in the saddle, my seat
   in the sky,
I'll quit punchin' cattle in the sweet by
   an by.

Come-a ti yi yippy, yippy,
   yay, yippy yay!
Come-a ti yi yippy,
         yippy, yay!

My Dog Rags

Elizabeth Deutsch
Evelyn Atwater
Sing 'n Do Co., Inc.

I have a dog his name is Rags; He

eats so much his tum - my sags, His

ears flip flop his tail wig wags, And

when he walks, he walks zig zag. He goes flip flop, wig wag,

zig zag; He goes flip flop, wig wag, zig zag; He goes

flip flop, wig wag, zig zag; I love Rags and he loves me!

My dog Rags he loves to play,
He rolls around in the mud all day.
I whistle, he won't obey,
He always runs the other way. CHORUS

Head and Shoulders

Additional lyrics:
Nancy & John Cassidy

G

Head and shoul-ders, knees and toes, knees and toes.

D7

Head and shoul-ders, knees and toes, knees and toes, and

G   **G7**   **C**   **A7**

Eyes and ears and mouth and nose,

D7   **G**   **C**   **G**

Head and shoul-ders, knees and toes, knees and toes.

Ankles, elbows, feet and seat, feet and seat;
Ankles, elbows, feet and seat, and feet and seat;
Hair and hips and chin and cheeks,
Ankles, elbows, feet and seat, feet and seat.

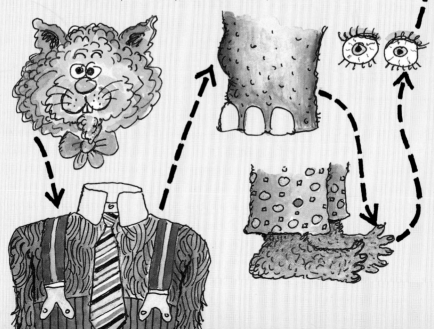

Rockin' Robin

J. Thomas

He rocks in the tree-tops all day long,

Hop-pin' and a-bop-pin' and a-sing-in' his song.

All the lit-tle bird-ies on J-Bird Street,

Chorus:

Love to hear the rob-in go tweet, tweet, tweet. Rock-in'

rob-in, (tweet, tweet, tweet); Rock-in'

rob-in, (tweet, tweedle-dee); Go rock-in' rob-in, we're

real-ly gon-na rock to-night.

42

Every little swallow, every chickadee,
Every little bird in the tall oak tree,
The wise old owl, the big black crow,
Flappin' their wings singin' go bird, go.

CHORUS: Rockin' robin (tweet, tweet, tweet)
         Rockin' robin (tweet, tweet, tweet)
         Go rockin' robin, we're really gonna rock tonight.

              The pretty little raven and the red-rock hen,
              talkin' how the robin was boppin' again,
              He started goin' steady and "bless my soul,"
              he out-bopped the buzzard and the oriole.

              CHORUS

He rocks in the treetops all day long,
hoppin' and a-boppin' and a-singin' his song.
All the little birdies on J-Bird Street,
love to hear the robin go tweet, tweet, tweet.

CHORUS

              Go rockin' robin, we're really gonna rock tonight.

43

Mail Myself to You

Woody Guthrie

I'm gon-na wrap my-self in pa-per,

I'm gon-na daub my-self with glue,

Stick some stamps on top of my head,

I'm gon-na mail my-self to you.

I'm gonna tie me up in a red string,
I'm gonna tie blue ribbons too,
I'm gonna climb up in my mail box,
I'm gonna mail myself to you.

When you see me in your mail box,
Cut the string and let me out,
Wash the glue off of my fingers,
Stick some bubble gum in my mouth.

Take me out of my wrapping paper,
Wash the stamps off of my head,
Pour me full of ice cream sodies,
Put me in my nice warm bed.

Repeat first verse.

44

45

Mrs. Murphy's Chowder

Traditional
Arrangement: N. Cassidy

Won't you bring back, won't you bring back Mrs. Mur-phy's chow-der? It was

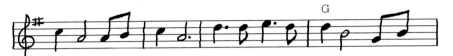

tune-ful, ev-'ry spoon-ful made you yo- del loud-er. Af- ter

din-ner Un-cle Ben used to fill his foun-tain pen From a

bowl of Mrs. Mur- phy's chow- der. Chorus: There was

ice cold ben-zine, gas-o Soup beans, string beans, float- all a - round.
cream, cream, line, ing

Sponge beef mis-take, stom- ache, cream ear man-y to be found.
cake, steak, ach puffs, muffs,

Silk hats, door mats, bed slats, Dem-o-crats, cow bells, door bells, beck-on you to dine.

Meat balls, fish balls, moth balls, can-non balls. Come on in, the chow-der's fine!

CHORUS:

There was ice cream cold cream, benzine gasoline,
Soup beans, string beans, floating all around.
Sponge cake, beef steak, mistake, stomach ache,
Cream puffs, ear muffs many to be found.
Silk hats, door mats, bed slats, Democrats,
Cow bells, door bells, beckon you to dine.
Meat balls, fish balls, moth balls, cannon balls.
Come on in, the chowder's fine!

Won't you bring back, won't you bring back, Mrs. Murphy's
    chowder.
It was tuneful, every spoonful made you yodel louder.
If they had it where you are, you might find a motor car,
In a bowl of Mrs. Murphy's chowder.

CHORUS

47

He's Got the Whole World in His Hands

Traditional
Additional lyrics: N. Cassidy

He's got the whole world — in his hands, He's got the

whole world — in his hands, He's got the whole world —

in his hands, He's got the whole world in his hands.

He's got my brothers and my sisters in his hands,
He's got my brothers and my sisters in his hands,
He's got my brothers and my sisters in his hands,
He's got the whole world in his hands.

He's got the sun and the rain, in his hands,
He's got the moon and the stars, in his hands,
He's got the wind and the clouds, in his hands,
He's got the whole world in his hands.

He's got the rivers and the mountains, in his hands,
He's got the oceans and the seas, in his hands,
He's got you and he's got me in his hands,
He's got the whole world in his hands.

He's got everybody here, in his hands,
He's got everybody there, in his hands,
He's got everybody everywhere, in his hands,
He's got the whole world in his hands.